CATS
LOOK-AND-LEARN

DORIS A. DE PRISCO
Photos by TETSU YAMAZAKI

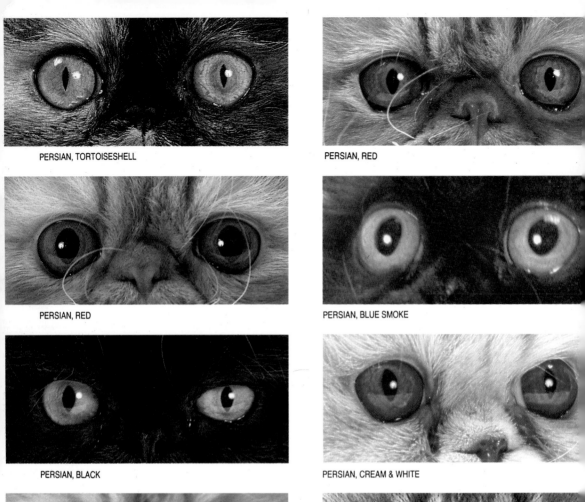

PERSIAN, TORTOISESHELL

PERSIAN, RED

PERSIAN, RED

PERSIAN, BLUE SMOKE

PERSIAN, BLACK

PERSIAN, CREAM & WHITE

PERSIAN, RED CLASSIC TABBY

NORWEGIAN FOREST CAT, BLUE MACKEREL TABBY

SIAMESE, BLUE LYNX POINT

PERSIAN, CHINCHILLA SILVER

NORWEGIAN FOREST CAT, BLACK

RAGDOLL, SEAL POINT

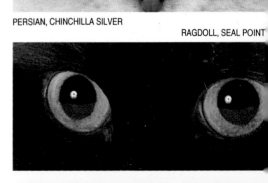

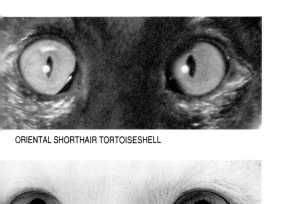

ORIENTAL SHORTHAIR TORTOISESHELL

NORWEGIAN FOREST, BROWN CLASSIC TABBY & WHITE

MANX, ODD-EYED WHITE

RUSSIAN, BLUE

SCOTTISH FOLD, TORTOISESHELL & WHITE

HIMALAYAN, SEAL POINT

NORWEGIAN FOREST CAT, BROWN, MACKEREL, TABBY & WHITE

NORWEGIAN FOREST CAT, BLUE MACKEREL TABBY

PERSIAN, BLACK

SCOTTISH FOLD, BLUE MACKEREL

PERSIAN, RED

MAINE COON, BROWN CLASSIC TABBY

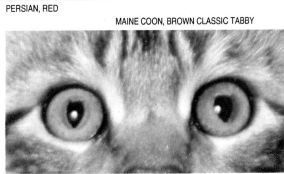

ABYSSINIAN

The Abyssinian originated in the African country of Abyssinia (now called Ethiopia). It was brought to England by British soldiers. The Abyssinian people considered this cat a symbol of God. Their customs regarded this cat as the child of the Egyptian pharaoh cats.

Cat lovers refer to this cat as the *ABY*, especially in the United Kingdom. The British cat lovers spread the breed worldwide. The first registered Abys showed up in 1896 and they have been popular ever since.

America had to wait ten years for the breed to cross the Atlantic Ocean. The first Abys showed up in 1906. They were offspring of British Abys. All cat associations recognize this breed and no outcrossing is allowed.

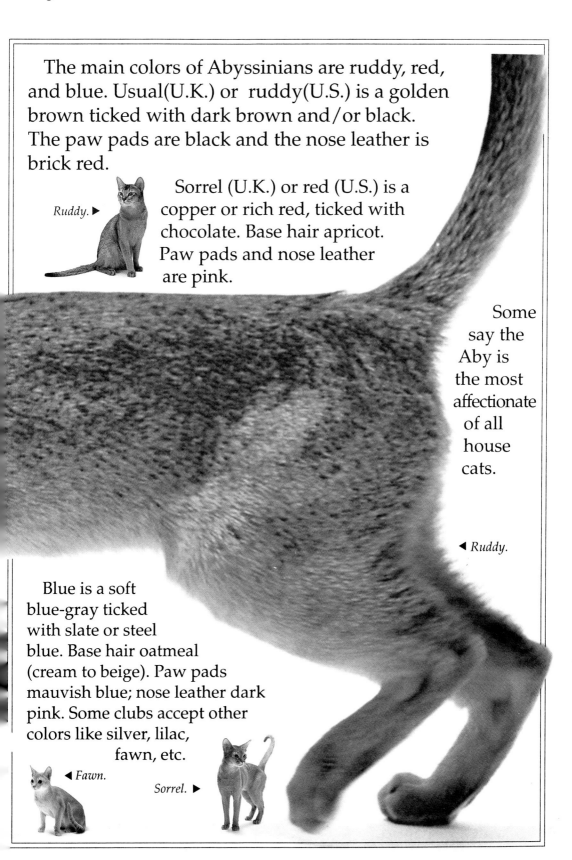

The main colors of Abyssinians are ruddy, red, and blue. Usual(U.K.) or ruddy(U.S.) is a golden brown ticked with dark brown and/or black. The paw pads are black and the nose leather is brick red.

Ruddy. ▶

Sorrel (U.K.) or red (U.S.) is a copper or rich red, ticked with chocolate. Base hair apricot. Paw pads and nose leather are pink.

Some say the Aby is the most affectionate of all house cats.

◀ *Ruddy.*

Blue is a soft blue-gray ticked with slate or steel blue. Base hair oatmeal (cream to beige). Paw pads mauvish blue; nose leather dark pink. Some clubs accept other colors like silver, lilac, fawn, etc.

◀ *Fawn.*

Sorrel. ▶

▼ *Blue.*

This lovely Aby is a blue male. It has the look of a sensitive, loving pet.

Abyssinians must have no bars on their legs, chest, or tail, even though there are faint markings often visible in kittens. Kinked or whip tails, extremes of type, incorrect eye color, white lockets and any white that extends beyond the lips to the neck are all serious faults. If you want a good Aby, check for these imperfections. While these problems affect the Aby's chances in the show ring they have NOTHING to do with their ability to be lovely pets.

▼ *Agouti.*

◄ *Ruddy.*

The Aby seems to have the general appearance of the African wildcat, *Felis silvestris.*

This is a champion quality sorrel Abyssinian. Even at less than one year of age it has become a Grand Champion.

◀ *Sorrel.*

Compare the young champion sorrel above with this mature ruddy Abyssinian female. She has the dignified poise and independent attitude for which cats are famous. Abyssinians are not a natural breed, and they are still in the process of development. It is almost certain that new color varieties will be developed. At the present time, it is a cat for the sophisticated connoisseur and may be expensive for a good quality kitten.

▲ *Ruddy.*

▼ *Red.*

This is the color which Aby fanciers call *red*, though it may not be the red color to which most cat fanciers are accustomed. This female is a Grand Champion. She was caught in this unnatural pose as she was about to move out of the photographer's view.

AMERICAN CURL

The ears of the American Curl are a recent phenomenon. Developed by genetic mutation, the American Curl breed began in California in 1981 and the breed occurs in both long and short haired varieties. Like its progenitor, the new breed occurs in most of the colors of the American Shorthair as well as lynx points more typically seen on the Siamese cats.

The Scottish Fold, a different purebred with unusual ears, is not related to the American Curl.

▲ American Shorthair.

It was the American Shorthair, however, that gave birth to this new breed. In a litter of regular Shorthair cats arose a special kitten with these new wonderful ears!

▼ Blue.

▼ *Seal lynx point.*

In body type the Curl is semi-foreign, which means it is neither cobby like its relative the American Shorthair, nor is it lean and long like the beautiful Siamese.

Black and white. ▲

◀ *Black.*

Faults in the breed include a kink in the tail, cobby or foreign type, woolly hair, drop or firm ears, and unmatched ears.

AMERICAN SHORTHAIR

Your everyday housecat in purebred form, the American Shorthair is the United States' version of the shorthaired cats on the Continent. In England, the cat is known as the British Shorthair; in Europe, the European Shorthair.

▲ *Silver classic tabby.*

The American Shorthair is believed to have accompanied the Pilgrims on the Mayflower. This is not a glamour cat, but a utility cat, originally transported to the Colonies to rid the supplies and homes of mice and other vermin.

The American Shorthair comes in a large variety of colors and patterns including white, black, blue, red, cream, bicolor, brown tabby, blue tabby, red tabby, silver tabby, cream tabby, patched tabby, calico, chinchilla, shaded silver, shell cameo, and smokes.

Even though the American Shorthair is your "average" cat, it must appear purebred through and through.

◀ Red classic tabby.

▼ Shaded silver.

Cream classic tabby.
▼

Any appearance of hybridization is a bad fault, as is a long or woolly coat—hence the name American Shorthair.

Eye color adheres to the coat color and is fixed genetically. Any diversions are considered faulty.

▼ *Brown classic tabby.*

▲ *Black.*

These are industrious and curious little cats, who are known for their affection as well as their intelligence.

Nothing exaggerated, this Yankee Doodle kitty is the original sensible feline!

▲ *Silver classic tabby.*

▲ *Red classic tabby.*

▲ Silver classic tabby.

▼ Silver classic tabby.

AMERICAN WIREHAIR

▲ *Calico.*

This unusual New York-born mutant sprang out of litters of American Shorthairs. The coat is described as crimped and hooked, not short and even like the Shorthairs.

This is a cobby cat, not foreign in type like the Rex breeds of cats, who have a similar coat type. Generally speaking, the American Wirehair is not a popular cat but is an undeniably intriguing purebred. It has been in existence since the mid-1960s.

Tortoiseshell. ▼

Unlike all the other mutant type cats, the American Wire-hair shows no side effects of its mutation. It is a most "normal" cat, if normal cats exist!

The colors of the American Wirehair are the same as the American Shorthair, but surely some colors are quite difficult to locate.

The coat is medium in length and springy; each hair of the coat is crimped, hooked or bent. The whiskers are desirably curly, though this is not common.

Calico. ▲

BALINESE/JAVANESE

Seal lynx point. ▼

The elegant, longhaired Balinese offers a fine, silky, medium-length coat without a dense undercoat. Its beautiful tail is plume-like though its face appears smooth coated.

This is a Siamese pointed cat who enjoys the foreign body type as well as the seal, blue, chocolate and lilac points. In some registries, other color points are acceptable. In the United States, these other colors are recognized as a separate breed, the Javanese.

Color points in both the Balinese and the Javanese occur on the face mask, ears, feet and tail. This is a medium-sized cat with a distinct expression.

▲ *Frost point.*

Its outgoing ways and attractive appearance derive from its progenitor the Siamese, a breed long adored for its near-human personality.

The Balinese and the Javanese are of unusually keen intelligence. Their easycare coat requires less brushing and maintenance than any of the double-coated cats who are longhaired. Like all other cats, these breeds are clean and mostly self-reliant.

Seal lynx point. ▶

Siamese fanciers never fancied the development of a longhaired Siamese cat. Surely certain early Siamese lovers would not be pleased to find not one but two (or more!) separate breeds of longhaired Siamese cats.

▲ *Lilac lynx point.*

Blue lynx point. ▶

When the Balinese first came on the scene it was called a Longhaired Siamese. Because the Himalayan also derived from the Siamese, the two breeds were confused for a time.

The Balinese and Javanese, whose distinction is solely color, are far more dainty and wedge-headed than the Himalayan, who is more full-bodied and cobby. Like the Persian and the Siamese, all these spinoff breeds have healthy and enthusiastic fancies.

▲ *Lilac point.*

While the Balinese will likely remain limited to the four original colors (in certain registries), the Javanese will continue to enjoy new colors and hues for as long as cats are popular.

BENGAL

The Bengal derives from crosses of domestic cats to the Asiatic leopard cat, *Felis bengalensis*. From that cat's scientific name does the hybrid get his name: Bengal. As with all other crosses to non-domestic cats, the progeny are semi-wild in appearance and possess a strong independence. First generation animals are rarely as tame as later generations.

▲ *Agouti.*

Presently these stunning felines are quite expensive. The closer to the Asiatic cat the more expensive the offspring will be. In order to maintain the desired level of wild cat, it is necessary for breeders to continue to use the Asiatic cats.

Leopard. ▶

Their colors are striking: leopard, golden and snow leopard.

BIRMAN

The legendary Sacred Cat of Burma, the Birman, has a beautiful silky coat pointed in Siamese cat fashion with sapphire blue eyes. Its points can be very light to very dark.

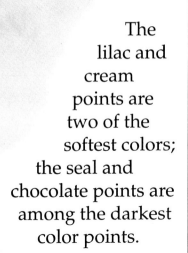

The lilac and cream points are two of the softest colors; the seal and chocolate points are among the darkest color points.

▲ *Lilac point.*

Colors include seal point, blue point, chocolate point, lilac point, red point, seal tortie point, cream point, blue tortie point, chocolate tortie point, lilac tortie point, seal tabby point, blue tabby point.

▲ *Seal point.*

Seal point. ▶

The points color the mask, ears, tail, and legs. The feet are desirably white.

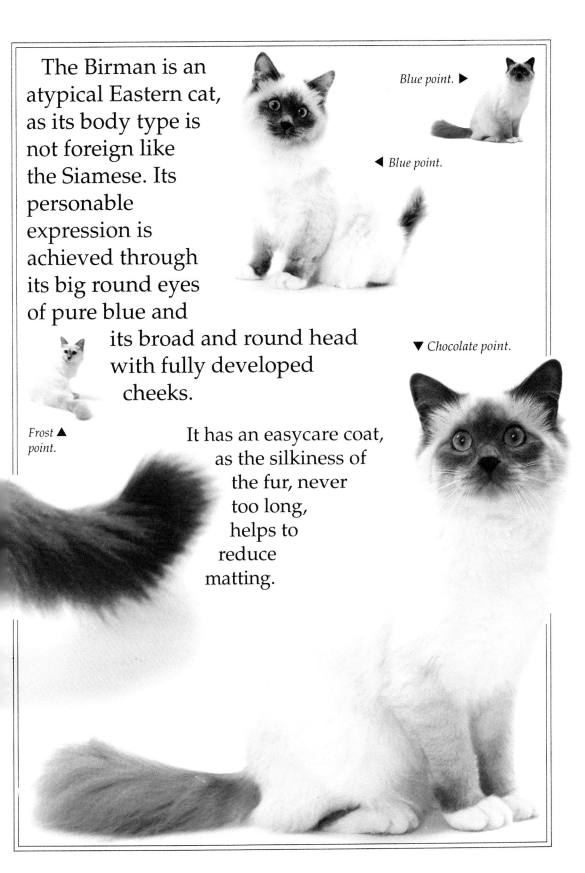

The Birman is an atypical Eastern cat, as its body type is not foreign like the Siamese. Its personable expression is achieved through its big round eyes of pure blue and its broad and round head with fully developed cheeks.

It has an easycare coat, as the silkiness of the fur, never too long, helps to reduce matting.

Blue point. ▶

◀ Blue point.

▼ Chocolate point.

Frost ▲ point.

BRITISH SHORTHAIR

The original stout-hearted cat, the British Shorthair is a no-nonsense domestic cat of England, the progenitor of America's own American Shorthair. These cats originated as the farm and street cats of the British people.

▲ *Blue.*

White. ▶

Blue. ▶

In England each color variety is viewed as a separate breed. The self colors include white, black, blue, chocolate, lilac, red; the tabby patterns include brown, silver, blue, red and cream; tortoiseshells in blue-cream, chocolate and calico; bicolors; pointed or Himalayan patterns; smokes and tippeds.

▼ *Bicolor.*

Like the American Shorthair, the British Shorthair is a utility-first cat, not exaggerated and a little smaller than the American breed.

Black. ▶

BURMESE

Originally a sable or brown-colored cat, the Burmese was derived from a brown cat that arrived in the United States from Burma in the 1930s and was crossed to a Siamese. It is a difficult cat to describe as the British cat folk prefer a more Oriental body type and Americans favor the more stocky cat. In America the cat is generally in the sable family, whereas in England other colors are acceptable such as cream, red and a variety of tortoiseshell patterns.

▲ *Chocolate.*

▲ *Champagne.*

▼ *Sable.*

◀ *Sable.*

▼ *Cream.*

In England the Burmese is a very popular cat, outnumbered only by Longhairs and Siamese.

▼ *Champagne.*

CORNISH REX

Unusual for its ripple-like coat, the Cornish Rex began in a litter of farm cats in Cornwall, England. The mutation for coat makes the breed unique, though it is similar to the Devon Rex, and affects the body type as well.

▼ *Red mackerel tabby.*

The original cats looked nothing like their cobby parents.

The Cornish Rex occurs in all coat colors and patterns, with or without white markings. When the Cornish Rex displays the pointed coat pattern, it is called the Si-Rex and may not have white markings.

▲ *Bicolor.*

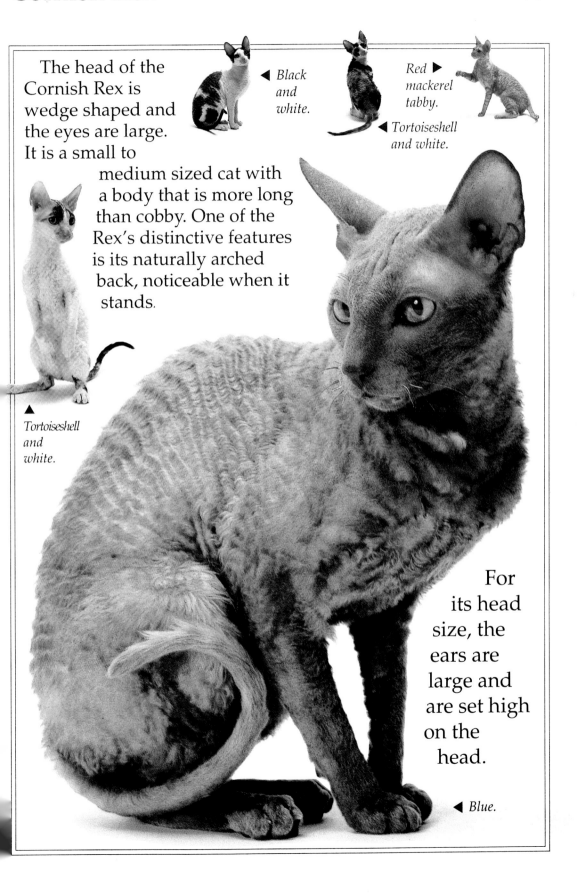

The head of the Cornish Rex is wedge shaped and the eyes are large. It is a small to medium sized cat with a body that is more long than cobby. One of the Rex's distinctive features is its naturally arched back, noticeable when it stands.

◀ *Black and white.*

Red ▶ *mackerel tabby.*

◀ *Tortoiseshell and white.*

▲
Tortoiseshell and white.

For its head size, the ears are large and are set high on the head.

◀ *Blue.*

DEVON REX

The second of the Rex variety cat breeds, the Devon Rex possesses a similar rippled coat, which is very short, soft and curly. The coat is not dense throughout but varies.

The whiskers are very brittle and tend to break.

The Devon comes in all colors and patterns, including the Si-Rex, which is patterned like a Siamese.

▼ *Blue.*

▲ *White.*

▼ *White.*

Today, the Rex type cats are gaining in popularity. In addition to the Cornish and Devon Rex, new breeds such as the Selkirk Rex have entered the fancy.

▲ *Brown mackerel tabby.*

White. ▶

Compared to the Cornish Rex, the Devon has a different face, described as pixie or elf-like with full cheeks and a modified wedge-like shape. The coats are only slightly different though they are two separate breeds.

If you breed a Devon Rex to a Cornish Rex, the offspring will have normal coats!

▲ *Brown mackerel tabby.*

EXOTIC SHORTHAIR

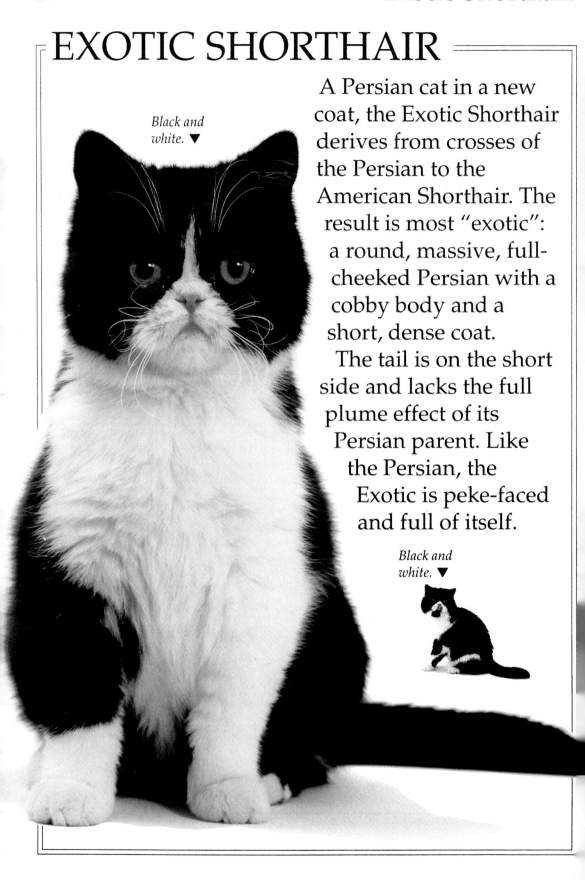

Black and white. ▼

A Persian cat in a new coat, the Exotic Shorthair derives from crosses of the Persian to the American Shorthair. The result is most "exotic": a round, massive, full-cheeked Persian with a cobby body and a short, dense coat.

The tail is on the short side and lacks the full plume effect of its Persian parent. Like the Persian, the Exotic is peke-faced and full of itself.

Black and white. ▼

In color the Exotic Shorthair can be found in every feline color and pattern (all those colors and combinations found in the American and British Shorthairs, as well as Persians).

▼ *Blue and white.*

The eyes, which correspond to the coat color, are round and large.

▼ *Blue.*

Blue. ▶

The beautiful Exotic Shorthair gains in popularity among Persian fanciers, who enjoy the new breed's Persian temperament and easycare coat. Persians require daily brushings while Exotics need to be brushed only a couple times each week.

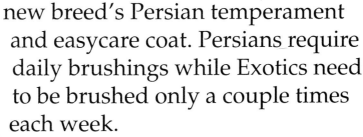

◀ *Blue.*

Black. ▶

HAVANA BROWN

The chestnut cat, the Havana Brown is a loving Siamese-like cat who takes its name from its coloration.

Although the coloration can be as light as frost and lilac, the original cats were black-brown. The variation in the color tone is due to the Havana's genetic make-up and some attribute the lighter tones to the Russian Blue.

Frost. ▶

▲ *Chestnut brown.*

Type varies from England to America, with the Americans favoring a more midway cat and the British preferring the long and svelte more classic Siamese body type.

Chocolate. ▶

▼ *Chocolate.*

The British breed more closely conforms to the standard of the Oriental Shorthair (chestnut). In England the breed is simply called Havana.

HIMALAYAN

▲ Tortie point.

The Colorpoint Longhair or Persian has been traditionally called the Himalayan, named for its specific coloration. The pointed pattern is commonly associated with the Siamese cat, from whom the breed began. The Siamese was crossed with the Persian to yield the Himalayan, essentially a Persian with Siamese coloration.

▲ Red point.

▼ Blue point.

◄ Red point.

Seal point. ▶

▼ Seal point.

In many cat registries today the breed is considered but a color variation of the Persian breed, and Siamese cats are never bred into an established Himalayan line. Most commonly Persians are used to maintain the desired cobby type.

Color points in the breed include seal, blue, chocolate, red or flame and cream, as well as tortie points, tabby points, and tortie tabby points. The body color adheres to the point color.

▲ *Seal point.*

Red point. ▶

JAPANESE BOBTAIL

The near tailless Eastern-born mutant known as the Japanese Bobtail is unique in the cat world. Unlike the Manx breeds, this breed's lack of a tail is not deemed an abnormality and is therefore

▲ *Black and white.*

safer to breed. Nonetheless the breed is not as popular as the Manx.

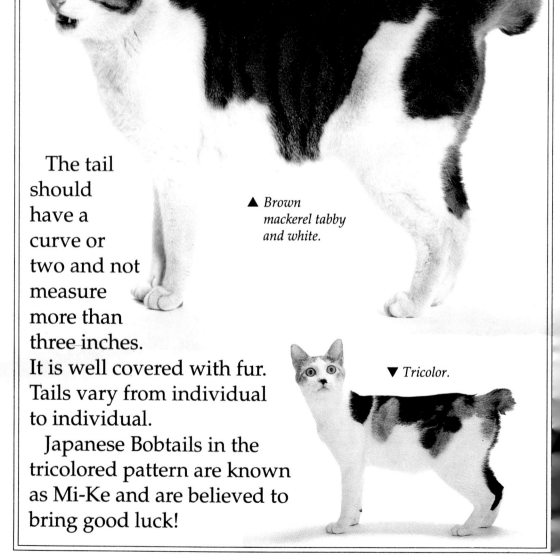

▲ *Brown mackerel tabby and white.*

The tail should have a curve or two and not measure more than three inches. It is well covered with fur. Tails vary from individual to individual.

Japanese Bobtails in the tricolored pattern are known as Mi-Ke and are believed to bring good luck!

▼ *Tricolor.*

KORAT

The Korat is a native cat to Thailand and is believed to be of ancient beginnings.

It is a semi-cobby cat with a distinct blue/gray coat, which appears to be tipped in silver. The standard describes the cat as any shade of blue.

▲ *Blue.*

In recent times the Korat is gaining in the popularity polls, though it is still considered quite rare.

In Thailand the Korat is called Si-Sawat and is considered a good luck charm.

▲ *Blue.*

MAINE COON

A natural outdoorsman, the Maine Coon cat boasts a thick, shaggy coat with a full complement of furnishings forming a ruff or bib, breeches, and mask hair. While the original Maine Coons were tabby in color the breed can be found in a variety of colors today.

Brown ▶
mackerel
tabby.

The Maine Coon must have a long thick tail which is very full and plume like, much like that of a racCoon!

▲ *Brown classic tabby.*

Red classic tabby and white. ▶

Brown ▶ *classic tabby.*

If ever any outdoor cat existed, the Maine Coon is it. The breed developed in the great outdoors, with little intervention from cat breeders. Today it is progenerated by cat breeders who give him a good home and an occasional forest romp.

◀ *Silver classic tabby.*

Brown ▶ *classic torbie.*

Brown ▶ *classic tabby and white.*

MANX

The real tail-free cat, the Manx comes to us from the Isle of Man off the coast of England. Mutations likely took place among this isolated group of cats and found favor with the Manx citizens as well as the British people.

Brown ▼
classic
tabby.

Breeding the Manx is very difficult and quite complicated due to the genetics involved. Only professionals should dare attempt breeding a Manx.

▼ *Black and*
white.

In the United States and Canada, there is a long-coated variety of the Manx known as the Cymric. This breed possesses all of the charms of its short-coated brother and offers a dense, all-weather coat.

▼ *Black and white.*

Many problems result in breeding these cats due to their lethal dominant gene. Manx colors and patterns are all inclusive, and in America the cats can also be shown with color points.

Healthy Manxes should be completely tailless and show no abnormality of the spine, hind legs or toes.

▲ *Odd-eye white.*

▼ *White.*

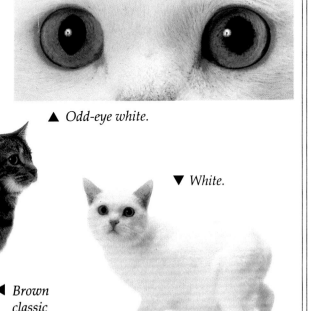

◀ *Brown classic tabby.*

NORWEGIAN FOREST CAT

A European-born longhair, the Norwegian Forest Cat remains a wondrous ancient feline of unknown origin. Its long, thick coat came through natural selection

Silver mackerel tabby.

as the original

Brown classic tabby. ▼

cats needed to survive Scandinavian winters. These were outdoor cats, or forest cats.

Not too many Norwegian Forest Cats can be found in either England or America as the breed's popularity has been limited by the greater availability of the Coon breed.

◀
Brown classic tabby and white.

Bown mackerel tabby and white. ▶

Red mackerel tabby. ▲

The Norwegian Forest can easily be confused with the Maine Coon cat, as both breeds enjoy a shaggy coat and a similar conformation. Norwegian Forest Cats are most commonly seen in tabby coat patterns, though in the United States fanciers have begun developing Norwegian Forest Cats in solid and pointed coats.

Blue torbie and white. ▶

Blue mackerel tabby. ▶

Brown mackerel tabby and white. ▼

ORIENTAL LONGHAIR

A natural outgrowth of the popular Oriental Shorthair, the Oriental Longhair is the longhaired elegant brother to that breed. It is not a broadly recognized cat breed though its popularity is growing. Like the Oriental Shorthair, from which this breed originated, the Longhair is an affectionate and outgoing feline.

▼ *Chocolate spotted tabby.*

The breed can occur in all colors excepting the pointed patterns. Due to the breed's newness, the entire spectrum of Oriental Shorthair colors are not likely available.

ORIENTAL SHORTHAIR

A solid colored Siamese (therefore non-pointed), the Oriental Shorthair is essentially self-colored, lithe and affectionate. Initially these cats were called Foreign.

▲ *Black.*

▼ *Frost.*

Oriental Shorthairs are usually as people-loving as their Siamese brothers, though some say they don't talk as much.

The breed can be found today in every color under the feline sun (except pointed), including tabbies, smokes and tortoiseshells.

▼ *Blue.*

▲ *White.*

PERSIAN

Shaded ▼
silver.

◄ Red.

Chinchilla
silver. ▼

◄ Cream.

The most popular cat in the world, the Persian is arguably the most beautiful as well! Having derived from cats of Turkey, today's felines possess bigger, denser coats, rounder faces and stockier bodies.

Shaded
golden. ▼

Persian colors span the rainbow of cat possibilities: self colors in black, white, blue, red, cream, chocolate, lilac; smokes in black, blue, red, tortie, cream, blue-cream, chocolate, lilac, chocolate tortie, lilac tortie; shaded in red, tortie, golden, silver, pewter; shell in cameo, chinchilla, chinchilla golden, tortoiseshell; bicolors; and tortoiseshell.

Tortoiseshell.
▼

◀ *Shaded silver.*

▼ *Black.*

The Persian's head is large and round with full cheeks. The nose is desirably foreshortened, called snub or peke-faced. The eyes are dramatic and large; the ears must be small and tipped.

Black smoke.▼

RAGDOLL

Seal point. ▶

The Ragdoll was created by cat fancier Ann Baker in the 1960s. It was originally registered exclusively with Baker's organization the International Ragdoll Cat Association. The breed even has a trademark. Its hallmarks are its deep blue eyes, color points, and mittens. There is also a bicolor Ragdoll.

Ragdolls love to be handled and prove to be very affectionate.

▲ *Seal mitted point.*

◀ *Seal mitted point.*

RUSSIAN BLUE

While the Russian Blue's origins can be traced to Russia, today's breed was revitalized by using the British Blue Shorthair and the Siamese. The cat's color is a clear blue with tipped silver guard hairs, creating a most unique effect.

▲ *Blue.*

◀ *Blue.*

The coat of the Russian Blue is remarkably dense. The breed is notably reticent and bonds closely with its owner. The breed is often compared to the Korat and the Chartreux, as well as the British Blue Shorthair. There are but minor differences.

▼ *Blue.*

SCOTTISH FOLD

The irresistible Scottish Fold derives from a mutation in farm cats in Scotland in the early 1960s. The mutation accountable for the breed's folded ears is responsible for certain other abnormalities in the cat, and the breed is therefore not accepted in Scotland.

▲ *Blue tortie and white.*

◀ *Calico and white.*

In the United States and England, the Scottish Fold is widely known, insomuch as a Longhaired version has also been promoted.

Brown classic tabby and white. ▼

▲
Brown classic tabby.

Blue mackerel tabby. ▼

The distinctive ears are neatly folded forward, desirably small and very tightly folded.

Colors of Scottish Folds are enormous with no limitations. Eye color should adhere to the coat coloration.

The unique earage of the Scottish Fold gives the breed a wonderfully endearing expression. Temperamentally the breed is a lovely companion animal.

◀
Brown classic tabby.

Blue mackerel and white. ▶

SIAMESE

◄ *Seal lynx point.*

The royal cats of Siam have enraptured cat lovers of the Western World for over a century. The Siamese is renowned for its elegant, lithe body, wedge-shaped head, and distinct markings.

Tortie point. ▼

Seal ► *point.*

Siamese keepers claim that the breed is abundantly affectionate and consistent in its likes.

The voice of the Siamese is unique and often in use!

▲ *Seal point.*

Chocolate point. ▲

Along with the Persian, the Siamese cat has been most influential on cat breeds. Siamese are the second most popular breed worldwide. They even appeared in the world's first cat show which took place in London in 1871. The Siamese reached New York about 1900. The Siamese takes its name from the previous name of Thailand which was Siam. Siam was teeming with cats to control rodents.

Along with the Siamese cat, Siam was host to the Korat and the Burmese. Cats are still very common in Thailand.

▲ *Seal point.*

SINGAPURA

Sepia ▶ agouti tabby.

▲ *Blue eyes.*

Sepia agouti tabby. ▼

The Singapura is the same as many street cats found throughout Asia, yet it is only the second cat that, as a natural breed, is recognized even though it has a ticked coat. The other natural breed is the Abyssinian. The Singapura was originally called the *drain cat* because it, like many cats in Malaysia, ate scraps which the local people threw into the streets and eventually washed into the street drains. All American cat registries recognize the Singapura, but the breed is very rare and, therefore, expensive. But they are worth it as they are very hardy, disease free, and friendly.

Sepia ▶ agouti tabby.

SNOWSHOE

The Snowshoe is a modern breed which has not really saturated the cat fancy with enthusiasts. It is basically a pointed breed with white feet. It was developed by crossing a Siamese with a bicolored American Shorthair. It is difficult to breed well-marked Snowshoes because of the great variation in feet markings.

◄ *Blue particolor point.*

The head shape of the Snowshoe is also variable, though the desirable shape is a modified wedge. The nose should be straight and in profile there is no stop. The eyes must be blue...no exceptions. The tail must be of medium length, tapering gently to the tip. There are just two acceptable colors: the seal point and the blue point.

Seal ► *particolor point.*

SOMALI

There is no universal agreement as to the origin of the Somali. The most logical argument is that it resulted from a cross of the Abyssinian strain with the Persian or some other longhair. Most of the cat fancy though believes that the cat originated as a sport amongst a litter of Abyssinians since there are longhaired Abys. There is no conformational difference between a Somali and an Aby except coat length. The breed is recognized by all cat organizations, some with slight modifications. The head should be modified, a slightly wedge shape.

◀ Fawn.

Fawn. ▶

The colors of Somalis are the same as for Abyssinians. Keep in mind that the ticked effect is not as apparent in this breed as in the Abyssinian due to the longer fur.

◀ Sorrel.

Ruddy. ▶

SPHYNX

Since its inception in the mid-1960s, the hairless Sphynx has come a long way. Hairless offspring, due to genetic mutations, have always occurred in mammals but were dismissed as freaks and culled. The Sphynx is unique in the cat world for its nakedness, and no other hairless breed has emerged.

The breed acts as normal as any cat, but needs some very special attention. Due to its lack of hair (near total absence, including almost no whiskers!), it needs to be safeguarded against cold weather with a sweater and kept out of the sun, as its skin can be burned easily.

For people who don't like the fur of cats, the Sphynx may be a miracle find!

Breeding the Sphynx is extremely complicated and must be left to the experts.

▲ *Blue classic torbie.*

▼ *Blue classic torbie.*

◄ *Red.*

TONKINESE

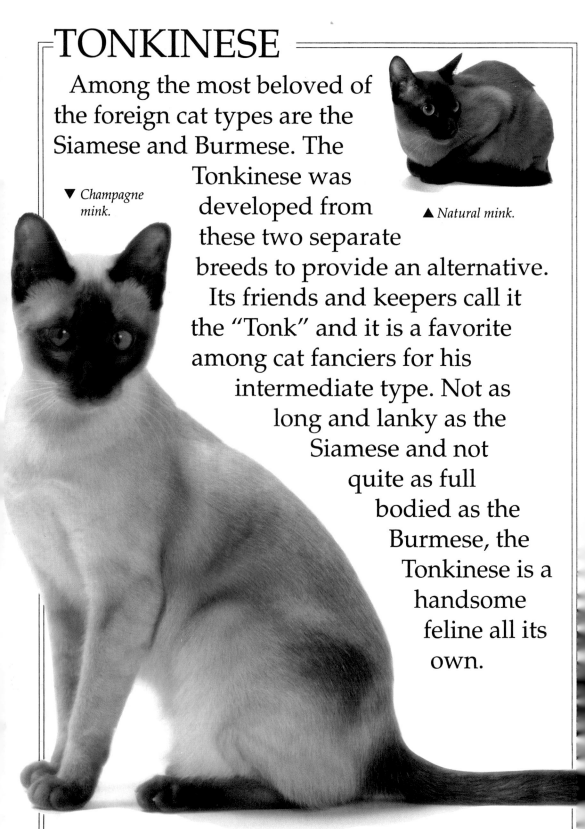

Among the most beloved of the foreign cat types are the Siamese and Burmese. The Tonkinese was developed from these two separate breeds to provide an alternative. Its friends and keepers call it the "Tonk" and it is a favorite among cat fanciers for his intermediate type. Not as long and lanky as the Siamese and not quite as full bodied as the Burmese, the Tonkinese is a handsome feline all its own.

▼ *Champagne mink.*

▲ *Natural mink.*

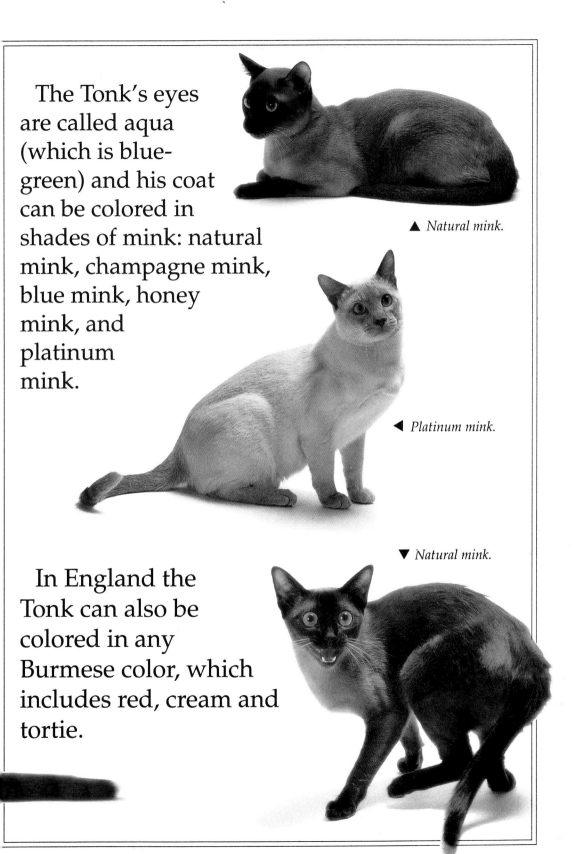

The Tonk's eyes
are called aqua
(which is blue-
green) and his coat
can be colored in
shades of mink: natural
mink, champagne mink,
blue mink, honey
mink, and
platinum
mink.

▲ *Natural mink.*

◄ *Platinum mink.*

▼ *Natural mink.*

In England the
Tonk can also be
colored in any
Burmese color, which
includes red, cream and
tortie.

TURKISH ANGORA

This lesser known breed is accredited for being the progenitor of the most popular of all cats, the Persian. The Turkish Angora, named for the Turkish capital city of Ankara, today has less coat than the Persian. Its coat is described as very fine and silky with a lovely sheen and minimal undercoat. On the ruff and undersides, the fur may be wavy.

Traditionally the breed was seen in solid white with blue, orange, green colored eyes or odd-eyed. Today the Angora can be seen in a variety of colors other than white.

▼ Blue.

▼ White.

TURKISH VAN

◀ *Red and white.*

The Turkish Van is a relative of the Turkish Angora and has gained notoriety as the cat that loves to swim. Its name "Van" describes its markings, which are auburn in color and found on the head and tail (often extending to rump). Cream marked cats can also be found today.

The Turkish Van is long in body but essentially of intermediate type, never as cobby as the Persian or American Shorthair and never as lanky and svelte as the Siamese.

The breed is on the move in the United States and England, and as any breed's popularity grows so too will the possible colors in that breed.

Red and white. ▶

INDEX

Distributed in the UNITED STATES to the Pet Trade by T.F.H. Publications, Inc., One T.F.H. Plaza, Neptune City, NJ 07753; distributed in the UNITED STATES to the Bookstore and Library Trade by National Book Network, Inc. 4720 Boston Way, Lanham MD 20706; in CANADA to the Pet Trade by H & L Pet Supplies Inc., 27 Kingston Crescent, Kitchener, Ontario N2B 2T6; Rolf C. Hagen Ltd., 3225 Sartelon Street, Montreal 382 Quebec; in CANADA to the Book Trade by Macmillan of Canada (A Division of Canada Publishing Corporation), 164 Commander Boulevard, Agincourt, Ontario M1S 3C7; in the United Kingdom by T.F.H. Publications, PO Box 15, Waterlooville PO7 6BQ; in AUSTRALIA AND THE SOUTH PACIFIC by T.F.H. (Australia), Pty. Ltd., Box 149, Brookvale 2100 N.S.W., Australia; in NEW ZEALAND by Brooklands Aquarium Ltd. 5 McGiven Drive, New Plymouth, RD1 New Zealand; in Japan by T.F.H. Publications, Japan—Jiro Tsuda, 10-12-3 Ohjidai, Sakura, Chiba 285, Japan; in SOUTH AFRICA by Multipet Pty. Ltd., P.O. Box 35347, Northway, 4065, South Africa. Published by T.F.H. Publications, Inc.

Manufactured in the United States of America by T.F.H. Publications, Inc.